# DIRK NOWITZKI

Dan Osier

PowerKiDS press.
New York

Fitchburg Public Library
5530 Lacy Road
Fitchburg, WI 53711

WITHDRAWN

READING POWER

Basketball's MVPs

Published in 2011 by The Rosen Publishing Group, Inc.
29 East 21st Street, New York, NY 10010

Copyright © 2011 by The Rosen Publishing Group, Inc.

All rights reserved. No part of this book may be reproduced in any form without permission in writing from the publisher, except by a reviewer.

First Edition

Editor: Amelie von Zumbusch
Book Design: Kate Laczynski

Photo Credits: Cover, p. 1 John Biever/Getty Images; p. 4 Glen James/ NBAE/Getty Images; p. 7 Ronald Martinez/Getty Images; p. 8 David Sherman/NBAE/Getty Images; p. 11 Randy Belice/NBAE/Getty Images; p. 12 Holger Sauer/Getty Images; p. 15 David E. Klutho/ Sports Illustrated/Getty Images; p. 16 Glenn James/NBAE/Getty Images; pp. 18–19 Noah Graham/NBAE/Getty Images; p. 20 (main) Greg Nelson/Sports Illustrated/Getty Images; p. 20 (inset) Nathaniel S. Butler/NBAE/Getty Images; p. 22 Doug Pensinger/Getty Images.

Library of Congress Cataloging-in-Publication Data

Osier, Dan.
 Dirk Nowitzki / by Dan Osier.
   p. cm. – (Basketball's MVPs)
 Includes index.
 ISBN 978-1-4488-2524-0 (library binding) — ISBN 978-1-4488-2632-2 (pbk.) — ISBN 978-1-4488-2633-9 (6-pack)
 1. Nowitzki, Dirk, 1978—Juvenile literature. 2. Basketball players—United States–Biography—Juvenile literature. I. Title.
 GV884.N69O85 2011
 796.323092—dc22
 [B]
                          2010023711

Manufactured in the United States of America

CPSIA Compliance Information: Batch #WW11PK: For Further Information contact Rosen Publishing, New York, New York at 1-800-237-9932

# CONTENTS

5

This is Dirk Nowitzki. He is a great
basketball player.

Nowitzki is 7 feet (2 m) tall. This helps him reach over other players.

**6**

Nowitzki most often plays power forward.

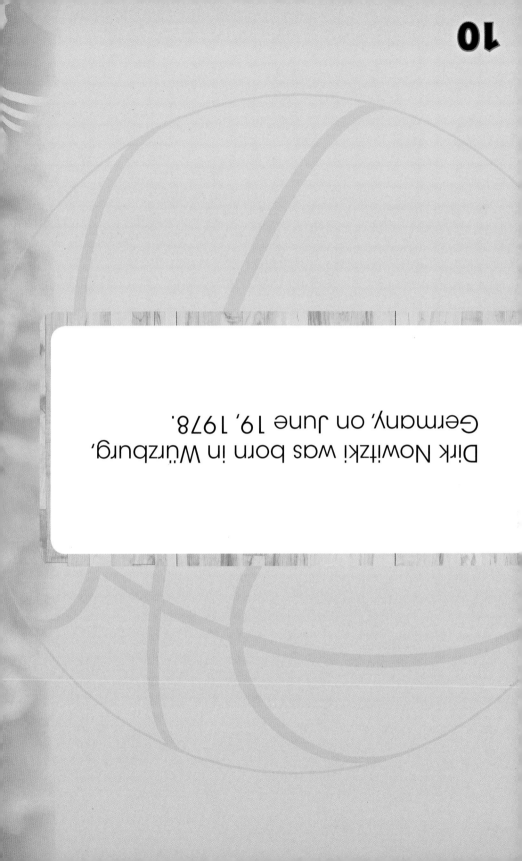

Dirk Nowitzki was born in Würzburg, Germany, on June 19, 1978.

Nowitzki played basketball in Germany as a teenager. He wanted to **join** the NBA, though.

In 1998, Nowitzki started playing for the Dallas Mavericks.

Nowitzki worked hard on his game. He learned a lot from his **teammate** Steve Nash.

Nash left the Mavericks in 2004. Nowitzki then became a team leader.

In 2007, Dirk Nowitzki was named the NBA MVP or most **valuable** player.

Today, Dirk Nowitzki has **fans** around the world!

# BOOKS

Here are more books to read about Dirk Nowitzki and basketball:

MacRae, Sloan. *Meet Dirk Nowitzki: Basketball's Blond Bomber*. All-Star Players. New York: PowerKids Press, 2009.

Zuehlke, Jeffrey. *Dirk Nowitzki*. Amazing Athletes. Minneapolis, MN: First Avenue Editions, 2007.

# WEB SITES

Due to the changing nature of Internet links, PowerKids Press has developed an online list of Web sites related to the subject of this book. This site is updated regularly. Please use this link to access the list:
www.powerkidslinks.com/bmvp/dirknow/

# GLOSSARY

**fans** (FANZ)  People who like a well-known person.

**join** (JOYN)  To come together or take part in.

**teammate** (TEEM-mayt)  A person who plays for the same team as someone.

**valuable** (VAL-yoo-bul)  Important.

# INDEX

P9-BBP-103